BEYOND ALL BELIEF

This book is published by
Grosvenor House Publishing Ltd
Link House
140 The Broadway, Tolworth, Surrey, KT6 7HT.
www.grosvenorhousepublishing.co.uk

Disclaimer
The author of this book does not dispense medical advice or prescribe
the use of any technique as a form of treatment for physical, emotional or
medical problems without the advice of a General Practitioner, either directly
or indirectly. The intent of the author is only to offer information of a
general nature to help you in your quest for emotional and spiritual wellbeing. In the event you use any of the information in this book for yourself,
the author and the publisher assume no responsibility for your actions.

A CIP record for this book
is available from the British Library

ISBN 978-1-78623-684-5

Also available in eBook format
ISBN 978-1-83975-024-3

BEYOND ALL BELIEF

A Living Bereavement
Understanding Estrangement and How to Survive It

DIANA DUNK

Grosvenor House
Publishing Limited

'Forgive the past. It is over.
Learn from it and let go.
People are constantly changing and growing.
Do not cling to a limited disconnected,
negative image of a person in the past.
See that person now. Your relationship is
always alive and changing.' Brian Weiss

To all those estranged

For my dearest son and grandsons in the hope that one day you will understand

and for Maria whose unfailing support and belief in me meant so much

Contents

Introduction

Beyond All Belief describes one woman's journey through life on her own, after being cast aside by her one and only child; a much loved son.

The estrangement affected her relationship with her grandchildren and other family members, but over time, she began to turn adversity into finding her own true worth, and her healing and recovery continue to be a work in progress. Through experiencing loss and grief, she is able to help comfort and support others faced with the despair of estrangement.

She found there was a common thread running through each narrative. Although different, they were all linked, in one way or another.

Beyond All Belief aims to help you understand the causes and stresses of estrangement and how you can take back control and find ways to live alongside it. Importantly, it shows how it is possible to turn your life around and make it worth living again.

'I have the choice of being constantly active and happy or introspectively passive and sad. Or I can go mad by ricocheting in between.' Sylvia Plath

This is not about adult children who were abused and neglected, but those who had a good relationship with one or both parents and were loved and cared for, up until the time they chose to alienate their parent.

I write from my own personal experience and some of the many distressing stories that parents have shared about the untold suffering caused by their estrangement from their adult child and grandchildren.

How do you deal with enforced separation brought about by your adult child? This happened to me over a period of years and, gradually, communication has more or less ceased.

My story of loss began over twenty-five years ago, on a two-week visit to see my newly married son and daughter-in-law, who were living and working in the United States. It was a hot, midsummer's day, and while they were out at work, I watered pots of wilted daisies on their veranda. My daughter-in-law's reaction was one of hysterical resentment, claiming it made her feel I was 'taking over.'

Estrangement doesn't happen overnight and, for me, it was gradual; a slow drip, drip, with a variety of incidents occurring along the way that helped estrangement and alienation take root and gather speed. Like a cancer, it spread silently through my family, corroding relationships as it went. It's what I call the 'ripple effect.'

It's an injury nobody sees. It goes unnoticed as we try to make sense of what is happening. Reeling from confrontational episodes, not knowing how much or how little to react; desperate to hold on to one's position as a parent and grandparent, but slowly losing your grip as you are cast aside.

At the same time, it becomes clear that no matter how hard others try, they don't fully understand what you are going through, or why. They tend to believe you must have done something to cause your adult child not to have anything further to do with you. In other words, in some way, you are to blame.

You feel guilt laden, a failure, and a parental responsibility for the breakdown. You try to analyse why and how your estrangement could possibly have happened.

'Grief is in two parts. The first is loss.
The second is the remaking of life.'
Anne Roiphe

Chapter 1

Estrangement

Estrangement is an enforced, hostile separation that causes acute pain and suffering to the recipient. It brings a plethora of raw emotions and uncertainties and, at the same time, a desperate intensity to remain ever part of your adult child's life. You feel utterly desolate, see no future, and wonder what will happen to you in your old age. Your adult child has purposefully walked away, withdrawing their love and affection, and often, they won't tell you why.

You become totally depressed; life seems hopeless, empty and devoid of all happiness. You're in limbo. Your social life lessens and you become introverted as you begin to lack confidence. Your health is compromised. Your energy levels plummet. I developed a throat condition which lasted a couple of years. I believe this was linked to my inability to 'speak up' for myself and ask for what I wanted. It was also caused by minimal and stilted communication with my son and not having anyone else I could speak to who would understand the suffering and family exclusion that faced me.

Starting my group, which supports parents and grandparents estranged from their families, has given me the opportunity to speak out and, I think, more importantly, be heard and receive much needed support. I no longer feel so alone.

Profound grief affects the immune system and it's hard to fight off viruses. Often, doctors are unable to find a specific cause for symptoms and treat you with medication rather than considering your emotional state and making a connection.

Although estrangement can happen at any point in your life, *Beyond All Belief* focuses on parents and grandparents who are forced to face this debilitating experience towards the latter part of their life. It's about parents who had a loving and caring relationship with their adult child throughout their childhood and adolescence, even though divorce might have affected the family unit.

Whether you are single or married makes no difference to estrangement, and if you have grandchildren, both grandparents can be severely emotionally and physically affected.

'Never be bullied into silence. Never allow yourself to be made a victim. Accept no one's definition of your life, but define yourself.'
Harvey Feirstein

It is how you deal with estrangement and alienation that is the crux of the matter, and whether you survive it or not.

Since founding the support group, I have met many estranged and alienated parents, all of whom have similar stories to tell, and all, without exception, are desperate to end their imposed exile and mend their severed relationships.

They are pining for their lost adult children and grandchildren. They are desperate in their quest to find a way to end their intense suffering and regain contact once again.

We are all at varying stages; some are starting out and alienation is new and raw, others have been estranged for many years. Some have never met their young grandchildren; others had a great deal to do with them and had developed a strong, loving and important bond before estrangement caused them to have minimal contact, or none at all.

Currently, in the United Kingdom, grandparents have no legal right to automatic access to their grandchildren. In the first instance, grandparents need to get permission from the Court to apply for a Court Order. If you decide to go down that route, it can be costly, drawn out, extremely stressful, and with no guarantee that your case will succeed. It can also mean that you risk damaging even further your already shattered relationship with your adult child.

It is hard to believe that your adult child would hold their own child to ransom; denying them the love and affection that they might otherwise receive from their grandparent. In this country alone, alienation is at epidemic proportions, with an estimated two million grandchildren being denied a loving relationship and access to their grandparents.

Will your adult child ever come to realise, through the fog of their deluded actions, the profound damage they are inflicting upon their own child, which can last a lifetime? That their actions colour their child's viewpoint regarding family unity, and the future relationships that they might have? How can they deliberately deprive their child of a loving relationship with their grandparents and all this can offer?

'Respond intelligently even to unintelligent treatment.' Lao Tzu

Some alienated parents live close to their adult child, which creates further heartache, as they are so near and yet so far. A grandmother once said she saw her grandchild every day on the school bus, but the child had been told not to speak to her. She said the grief she felt had ripped her heart out. Others live a long way away and so are out of sight and out of mind. Either way, the chances of reconciliation or forging any kind of meaningful relationship remain remote. Many elderly grandparents have very young grandchildren, some of whom they've never met, and they are acutely aware that the clock is ticking.

What estranged parents experience
- They won't talk to me
- My adult child is mind controlled
- I'm told I am to blame but they won't explain what I have done
- They require an apology for grievances held against me
- They refuse to meet and talk
- They ignore any offer of professional mediation

- They won't answer my emails and texts
- They don't send Christmas, birthday or Mother or Father's Day cards
- They withhold their address
- When they moved house, I wasn't given new contact details
- I miss out on important anniversaries as I'm never invited
- I was totally ignored at a family wedding
- I never attend a school prize day or concert
- I don't receive family photographs
- I send cards and presents but I don't know if my grandchildren get them
- All correspondence to my adult child goes unacknowledged
- I'm not allowed my grandchildren's mobile numbers or email addresses
- Envelopes of thank you notes from my grown-up grandchildren continue to be written by their mother
- I've been told my estranged adult child never wants to see me again
- I've been told I don't exist in their eyes
- I've been told my grandchild doesn't want to see me
- My grandchildren have never come to stay
- It's like I'm the enemy but I don't know why
- I've never met my grandchild
- The landline is permanently on ansaphone
- Grandchildren are withheld as punishment
- The adult child or partner is in control
- Hurt is all about the adult child; hurt to the estranged parent is ignored
- Extended family won't talk about it
- Extended family sides with the alienator

'The most valuable possession you can own is an open heart. The most powerful weapon you can be is an instrument of peace.' Carlos Santana

The casualties of estrangement, beside yourself, are your grandchildren, and remarkably, your adult child will ask you to 'respect' their decision in denying you access to them!

Grandchildren go through their formative years not knowing why they don't have both sets of grandparents in their lives, and they are rarely told the real reason why. They know we exist but don't know why we are not there for them. It's a huge disservice that their parents do, to the children they say they love.

My grandchildren were forbidden, throughout their childhoods, from contacting me using their mobiles or via email. I was told I should not go to their school or attend sports matches they were playing in, as only parents, not grandparents, attended them! It was an effective way of minimising and controlling communication between us.

They were cheated out of ever staying with me in my home and I have never spent any time alone with them.

The restrictions forced upon them have resulted in them not knowing how to have a natural relationship with their paternal grandmother. They have little idea how to relate to me, having had very few opportunities to do so, during their growing up years. Although there are signs of a willingness to connect, they are still hesitant, despite now being young men, and it's apparent the constraints that were imposed upon them from an early age remain, in part. In time, I hope that these insecurities will fade and they will feel more relaxed about getting to know their grandmother.

What estranged grandchildren and grandparents miss out on

- Unconditional love
- Having the time to do things together
- Special outings
- Sharing their dreams and aspirations
- Knowing your grandparents are there for you
- Sleepovers
- Sharing in their achievements
- Memories
- A special relationship
- A strong, loving and caring bond
- Relaying pearls of wisdom

*'Your pain is the breaking of the
shell that encloses your understanding.'
Kahlil Gibran*

Chapter 2

Alienation

Alienation by your adult child is heart-rending, malicious and cruel. To intentionally treat your parent with total indifference and to show no concern for their wellbeing is simply unconscionable.

It represents extreme emotional abuse, as it is knowingly inflicted. The disquieting disbelief that they have no regard for you is searingly painful. Their childhood and the love you gave them apparently no longer means anything. It's like those times never happened. You've been deliberately cast out of their life and treated as if you are worthless.

If a friend or acquaintance acted so callously, you wouldn't want to have anything to do with them, but when your son or daughter alienates you, the emotional turmoil is agonising.

You're caught in a catch-22 situation. In confronting your adult child, you risk never-ending antagonism and no hope of any kind of future relationship. If you keep quiet and don't confront them, the hostility continues, unabated. When you love someone, it's human nature to never give up hope, and believe that someday, somehow, it will come right, but in reality, it's not necessarily so.

Alienation takes away your status as a parent and grandparent. It is demoralising. Your opinions and advice don't count and are not welcomed. Any wisdom learned goes unrecognised, along with life skills that you might have gained. You have become superfluous, in their eyes. The future is bleak for an alienated parent, as you're on your own.

Alienation is like living through a cold war. There is an emotional distancing; a cessation of communication. Those who are supposed to support you don't, and those who should be on your side are not.

Alienation is not only about losing a loved one, it's about being on a journey not of your own making. To survive it, it's imperative that you change the goalposts and turn what is truly an undermining of your self-esteem, a stain on your character, a belittling of all you stand for, into knowing your own self-worth and becoming a confident, emotionally healthy individual who, once again, can embrace all that life offers.

Alienation is about another person projecting their inadequacies upon you in a quest to prove that somehow you don't matter. They are all-important. They don't care if it destroys you; it is of no importance, as long as they are seen by others as being in the right. They crave confirmation so that they can justify their unjustifiable actions.

You should never underestimate how far someone who feels in competition with you will go to weaken your status within the family. They are never satisfied, nor do they stop, until they have banished you from their life and, more importantly, from the lives of your loved ones. Their aim is to leave you in a barren wasteland with your family poisoned against you.

Your extended family can be a haven or a hell, depending on whether they choose to support you or leave you on your own to deal with the fallout of estrangement.

Family members are quite capable of taking sides. This depends on their own relationship and how they see their position within the family. Often, they make judgements based on partial facts and, in doing so, can create further tensions for you and with other family members.

'Those who know do not speak. Those that speak don't know.' Lao Tsu

Chapter 3

Support Group

Joining a support group for alienated parents and grandparents can give you an opportunity to express your grief, frustration, anger, desperation and bewilderment; all the raw emotions that you have kept hidden, believing there has to be something wrong with you, as you can't manage to have a normal relationship with your family.

Before joining a group, many parents and grandparents think they are the only ones who are estranged. It brings embarrassment and shame, and they don't want to speak about it, as they try to work out what they have done to cause the breakdown.

At first, family and friends are sympathetic, but quite soon, they begin to tire of hearing about your estrangement and depressive state. Estranged parents can spend hours alone in the depths of despair, not knowing how to change their circumstances. They are desperate to speak to their adult child and see their grandchildren.

Meeting others who are going through the same anguish and finding that whatever you say is met with understanding, combined with compassion and a genuine concern for your distress is empowering. I have been told by parents that the support they received helped save their life, as they had been feeling suicidal.

For some, it can be very difficult to take the first tentative step in helping themselves, as rejection has caused them to lose all self-esteem and confidence. As they gradually gather up courage to talk about their experiences and share them with other injured parents, they discover a new-found strength to handle alienation in a much more constructive and positive way.

They come to realise that they are not bad people; just ordinary people trying hard to deal with a complex situation. They learn to trust themselves, knowing the group is there for them. Having the additional opportunity to speak to or meet up with members in between meetings helps further the healing process.

Many of my friends and acquaintances had never heard of alienation by an adult child and only became aware of it when my relationship with my son and daughter-in-law became estranged. They had never come across somebody like me. It was difficult for them to grasp what had happened as, inevitably, many people believe it takes two to tango.

'We cannot change anything until we accept it. Condemnation does not liberate, it oppresses.' Carl Jung

Chapter 4

Mind Game

.

It's a mind game they play. Many parents, including myself, are told, 'If you don't know what you've done, I'm not going to tell you.' Usually this means there is another reason for their rejection of you and, more often than not, it has little to do with you. Your adult child may feel they need to appease their partner after pressures and influences have been placed upon them to stop seeing or speaking to you. However, there are times when you should not fully blame their partner, because your adult child – unless they've been mind controlled – has a mind of their own, and it's their choice to keep in contact or not. They know you are out there.

Some adult children demand you say sorry, even though you don't know what you're apologising for! Why is it that WE have to say sorry, but they feel no need to apologise to US, despite their deplorable behaviour? They initiated the estrangement; we did not. At the beginning of my experience, I found that saying sorry to appease them made no difference at all and was never acknowledged!

In many cases, it's not reconciliation the adult child seeks, but an admission of guilt, on your part, to give credence to their distorted actions, thus enabling alienation to go unchallenged and unabated. The adult child or partner's portrayal of you can be so convincing that it easily sways friends and family, bringing sympathy and support which reinforces belief in their embellished or fabricated story.

Frequently, your 'behaviour' is discussed by your adult child or partner with one or more family members, who are often sympathetic to them, as they don't want to risk falling out themselves. Because of this, family members are unlikely to question the given motive or version of events and it becomes an effective way of isolating you and making way for your adult child or partner to control the whole family.

'Follow your heart, listen to your inner voice,
stop caring about what others think.'
Roy T. Bennett

Chapter 5

Self-image

Self-image is built upon a person's perception of reality and it is influenced by how they think others see them.

Self-image is important to the adult child and partner and they will go out of their way to be seen as blameless victims. They show themselves as caring individuals, in contrast to the real dynamic of estrangement:

- The adult child insists the estrangement was caused by the parent, not them
- The adult child expects the parent to apologise for all the grievances that they continue to hold against them
- The adult child believes they have no responsibility in working towards an improved situation; the parent should be the bigger person
- Hurt is all about the adult child; hurt to the parent is ignored
- Estrangement is instigated by the adult child, then non-negotiable complaints follow

'Holding on to anger is like grasping a hot coal with the intent of throwing it at someone else; you are the one getting burned.'
Gautama Buddha

Chapter 6

Disowned

The loss of your living child is never expected, as we naturally believe they will remain loving, loyal and in our lives forever. The realisation that you are now disowned brings shock, disbelief, confusion and a profound sadness that spills over into every aspect of your life. The painful period of adjusting to your adult child's indifference can span many years, and often parents find it practically impossible to deal with.

As blame and wounding dialogue continue, they increase the anguish and can produce a hostility which escalates rather than dissipates. Where there is no improvement in the relationship, silence often reigns.

The harm caused, over time, is profound, and if at any point there is talk of reconciliation, restoring trust is not easy. When a parent has had to use the coping mechanism of trying not to care, simply to survive the fallout of alienation, how is it possible to restore confidence in a new-found offer of closeness?

In the past, I suggested mediation to break the deadlock, but it fell on deaf ears. It was apparent that neither my son nor daughter-in-law wanted to end the estrangement. Mediation meant they would need to commit to a level playing field of negotiation, which, apparently wasn't acceptable to one or both.

Another effective way to distance you from their lives, besides emotionally, is physically. When considering moving nearer to them, so that I could see them and my grandchildren and babysit when needed, I was told the closest I should be was half an hour's drive away, and I would never be needed to babysit. I didn't realise it at the time, but these were the seeds of alienation and what was to come.

'No one can make you feel inferior without your consent.' Eleanor Roosevelt

Chapter 7

Friendships

Friendships are fraught with pitfalls as most friends don't 'get' it. When you first talk about your estrangement, they are sympathetic and naturally ask what caused it. They expect a simple answer, as they refuse to believe that your son or daughter could possibly shut you out of their life without a reason.

Wanting a straightforward answer, they question your logic, but when nothing is forthcoming, it leaves an uncertainty that lingers in the air; a doubt that what you've described cannot be true. 'There must be more to it than that. It MUST be something you said or did!' they exclaim.

You are given advice on what to do and how to act when you see or speak to them, and you are told to pretend all is normal and just 'carry on.' They advise you to write and simply say that you want to see them, or to invite them to visit you. They tell you to be patient as 'they'll come around eventually. It's just a blip.'

They say you must continue offering the olive branch, no matter how many times they don't respond or refuse to meet you halfway. 'There has to be a way of changing their minds!' you are told, and it's inferred that YOU are not doing enough to break the deadlock. You're made to feel that it is up to you to change THEIR behaviour and that YOU are the one responsible for the impasse!

They won't accept that your adult child has intentionally decided not to have anything further to do with you. As time goes on, all mention of your estrangement fades and conversation returns to the normality of everyday life. It's a less confrontational place for friends to be.

'If you are still looking for that one person who will change your life, take a look in the mirror.' Roman Price

Chapter 8

Depression

Depression can be extremely difficult to overcome and I have found that the longer estrangement continues, the harder it is to navigate your way through it.

Depression is made up of isolation, sadness, loneliness, hopelessness, anxiety and guilt, and the feeling that nothing matters can overwhelm you at any given time. It comes with a sense of incredulity that life has come to this and not knowing what to do as an empty future faces you. Your emotions become a rollercoaster; one day up and the next day descending into the depths of depression.

You can be home alone or in a crowded place, but nothing prepares you for the all-encompassing feeling of isolation and the lack of real meaning to your everyday life. You see families with happy, smiling faces, interacting with each other. 'Why can't I have this?' you say to yourself, 'Where did I go so wrong?' The hard part is you didn't, and there is no answer.

Estrangement has happened and it looks as if it's here to stay; you have to find a way to replace your loss with something worthwhile. To mend the shattered pieces of your life, you need to gather up all your resources when you least feel like it.

At times like this, joining a support group can be a lifeline. Speaking to a trusted friend can help lift you out of the dark place you find yourself in.

Visiting your doctor might be the first step, for some. Others may find joining a Pilates, Yoga or Tai Chi class gives them a sense of wellbeing, along with exercise and the opportunity to make new friendships with like-minded people. Join a meditation group for calmness and grounding.

Think about a creative group such as musical appreciation, a writing or reading group. Join a dance class, start painting, or join a walking club; any kind of group that you will be part of and in which you are welcomed by people who take you at face value.

Consider a class where you might learn new skills which will help you to feel productive, or help others less fortunate than you (yes, there are some!) by volunteering.

If you love animals, help out at a rescue shelter or get involved with an animal charity seeking to bring an end to worldwide animal cruelty.

Consider giving a loving and secure home to a dog or cat in need, as they can be a great source of comfort.

If it's possible, spend time in the countryside, where nature offers a calming effect, and take time to notice the wonder of the four seasons. The friends you do have; nurture and value them and spend as much time as you can enjoying their company.

'When you love someone, you love the person as they are, and not as you'd like them to be.'
Leo Tolstoy

Those who feel all is lost, who don't have the will or energy to pick themselves up, should seek medical advice as soon as possible. Antidepressants can be prescribed and counselling sessions sought. Nationally, there are the Samaritans and Cruse loss and bereavement support groups that you could turn to for immediate help.

I've known grandparents who were suicidal, who spoke about walking into the sea to end it all, as they saw no hope, only a hollow future. They felt completely destroyed by their imposed alienation and the additional loss of their grandchildren's presence in their life. No adult child who has blocked you from your family is worth dying for.

Many estranged grandparents dread having to talk about or listen to a friend enthusing over their newborn grandchild. Having to look at family photographs or hear how their grandchildren are thriving is painful, as it amplifies our own loss. Having to sound enthusiastic while they describe the fun times they spend with them, the family birthdays they're invited to, the holidays they're part of, magnifies our sense of abandonment, which increases our despondency. Overwhelming feelings of longing spring up, adding a further layer to our desolation.

Estranged grandmothers often find attending friends get-togethers intolerable when conversation turns to news about grandchildren, family activities and supportive family members.

Alienation brings deep pain and suffering to the person caught in its crossfire, as it represents an ambiguous loss. Your adult child and grandchildren are absent from your life, but very much alive in your heart and mind. There can be no closure, because there has been no death, no passing, and that is one of the curses of alienation. It is a living bereavement.

There is a worldwide alienation epidemic, which is evidenced by the outpouring of stories posted on the worldwide net by parents and grandparents, and by the increase in much needed support groups that are annually growing in number. We are slowly realising that we are not alone.

Every story differs and some parents simply can't cope and become severely depressed, with feelings of utter despondency. Others manage to fill their lives with optimism and have found ways to make the most of every day.

'Turn your wounds into wisdom.'
Oprah Winfrey

Chapter 9

Speak Your Truth

One positive step is to be open with those you come into contact with. If asked about your family circumstances, be straightforward and tell it as it is: you are estranged, and because of this, prevented from having a relationship with your adult child and grandchildren.

Speak about how detrimental it has been to your life, and how you are trying to do your best on a daily basis. Tell them if you are part of a support group and explain how it helps you get through the dark, despairing times.

Be honest about what has happened to you. There is no need to feel ashamed, keep your estrangement a secret or feel the need to justify your position. You may find you are speaking to another estranged parent or, in all probability, they know somebody else who is.

When you sense that people may doubt your narrative, consider distancing yourself from them, as it's important to protect and nurture your own wellbeing. Surround yourself with as much positive energy as possible.

Negative vibes will drain and break you down, preventing you from healing the wounds that have been forced upon you. Learn to keep your own counsel. You own your truth.

'To thine own self be true.'
William Shakespeare

Chapter 10

The Blame Game

Blame between two parties is just different sides of the coin. To help prevent the fanning of flames, we need to look in a detached way and consider why they blame us.

Often an adult child won't stop to think about how the breakdown has occurred. They are not sure of the underlying causes, which prevents them from being objective and, because of this, their arguments are rarely logical. Blaming us saves them from having to take any responsibility for their own actions. It is an excuse not to deal with the real cause of the problem.

It could be as minor as a negative reaction to something once said, which is blown out of all proportion until it becomes a major issue and an effective prop for blame. They may not realise it, but blame begins to control them. It takes them over, every time they think of you; blaming more and more until they are blinded by their own negative emotions and can't think straight, where you're concerned. To other people, they will act normally, but to them, psychologically, you represent a lit match.

Blame is one of the most injurious of emotions. It destroys relationships, health and the future. It is a defence mechanism that gives the alienator a reason not to face their anxieties; to ignore their own flaws and insecurities and to find comfort quickly.

'Blaming things on the past does not make them better.' Nelson Mandela

What you can do

The way for us to combat blame is to let go of the need to blame them for their immature behaviour and choose empathy instead of judgement.

Break the cycle by staying in the present moment; don't spend time thinking about the past or the future, which will send you into a depressive downward spiral, fast.

Only the present moment can offer you the good things in life, through worthwhile friendships, helping less fortunate people or joining an activity group which will help give you the confidence and self-esteem that has been eroded. Be pro-active and get motivated. It's hard to do, but the rewards are there for the taking.

'You have power over your mind – not outside events. Realise this, and you will find strength.' Marcus Aurelius

Chapter 11

Passive-aggression

Passive-aggression is a method of dealing with people. Most passive-aggressive individuals have four common characteristics:

- They are unreasonable to deal with
- They're uncomfortable to experience
- They rarely express their hostility directly
- They repeat their subterfuge behaviour over time

Passive-aggression represents indirect anger shown by somebody who doesn't know how to express their feelings honestly and openly.

Often, we are presented with passive-aggressive behaviour by our adult child or their partner, which is very hard, if not impossible, to deal with. It represents hidden resentments; secretly trying to assert control over you or a situation. They believe they are in the right and will do anything to disparage you in not accepting their reasons for their actions.

A passive-aggressive person has low esteem and they knock you down in order to elevate themselves. If an adult child or their partner doesn't feel in control – perhaps they feel jealousy towards you – this goes hand in hand with the victim mentality. They don't know how to respond appropriately when someone is upset or defensive. Buried feelings of inadequacy make them feel they're not recognised, that they come second in their partner's eyes, and that you matter and they don't. They subtly undermine and sabotage you, all the time making out that they like you. They do not have your best interests at heart. They hate to be 'found out.' If you make requests or demands on them, they will often view these as unfair or unjust, and rather than express their feelings at the time, they cover them up and continue to resent you.

A great deal of passive-aggressive behaviour comes from the inability to communicate, coupled with a need for approval. A passive-aggressive person wants to see an overreaction by you, so that they can turn it into your 'unreasonable' behaviour.

Sullen behaviour is also a factor, as it makes them feel better about themselves if they can find fault with you and your ideas and beliefs.

Passive-aggressive people know only too well how hurtful it is to be left out of a family gathering. They know they can quietly ignore you and nobody else will notice; unless it is overtly done, making others feel awkward. Passive-aggression is subtle and easily missed.

If you ask why you are being ignored, a response will be denied and you will be seen as being confrontational, thus giving the passive-aggressive person their intended result.

They need to feel they have the upper hand and they have an unwillingness to end disputes. Their anger comes out in a passive way, as avoidance and withdrawal.

Particularly stressful is being on the receiving end of a passive-aggressive person. It is a form of indirect manipulation and dishonesty and can destroy relationships.

'Anger ventilated often hurries towards forgiveness; and concealed often hardens into revenge.' Edward G. Bulwer-Lytton

Parents who have a passive-aggressive adult child or an adult child who has a passive-aggressive partner

In a relationship where one partner displays passive-aggressive behaviour, it makes for an unhappy union. One of the many traits is disguised relational hostility. This includes the silent treatment, the invisible treatment, social exclusion, neglect, sullen resentment and indirectly hurting someone of importance to their partner.

For your adult child to accept that their partner is operating within a passive-aggressive pattern is painful. Often the passive-aggressive partner will feign loyalty and be accommodating.

If your adult child has got to the stage where they've noticed that their passive-aggressive partner finds ways to sabotage and undermine any close relationship they might have, it's time for them to trust their instincts and accept the reality of the situation.

As long as your adult child remains complicit by deliberately ignoring and inwardly justifying their partner's behaviour, it will continue, unabated. In the case of someone else noticing and pointing it out to them, they should not try to make excuses and explain it away.

It hurts deeply to accept that a partner has passive-aggressive tendencies and doesn't have your best interests, or those of the people you care for, at heart.

Once your adult child has become aware of the dynamics of their personal relationship, they must start taking steps to set boundaries that protect them from further passive-aggressive behaviour.

Depending on the severity of the issue, they may have to start being selective about what they share with their partner. Deep thoughts, feelings and aspirations might not be safe to express. They should use their judgement in order to go forward. They may find that only certain topics need to be off-limits, rather than a broad change to their communication being required. It's critical they protect themselves.

'Remember: nobody said it would be easy.'
Maxime Lagace

What you can do

Remember, any passive-aggressive behaviour directed at you is not about you. Knowing this can help to reduce the negative impact.

Maintain your composure and don't become hostile, as this will simply exacerbate the situation and they can identify you as the problem.

Try to keep your anger in check and point out their feelings towards you in a way that is non-judgemental, yet factual.

Step back and refuse to be drawn in, as it takes two to play this game. Don't be pressurised into accepting responsibility for everything.

Remember: you can't change the way they are, but you can change the way you respond to them. Respond rather than react, so that they are not controlling your behaviour, which is their aim.

'Hate is not conquered by hate. Hate is conquered by love. This is a law eternal.'
Gautama Buddha

Chapter 12

The Silent Treatment

Although the silent treatment is part of passive-aggression, it is different and something that countless parents and grandparents encounter with their adult child and partner.

I think it's important to mention, as it is very undermining. It's a weapon of choice and easy to get away with. They make out that they're taking the moral high ground, but in actual fact, this is a highly effective way of punishing and causing you pain.

When you are on the receiving end of the silent treatment, you realise, but often not immediately, that they hold a grievance against you and have no intention of telling you what it is. When you ask them to talk to you, they either don't reply, or they say, 'Nothing is wrong.' They know the anxiety that silent treatment causes and they want to use your discomfort to get your attention so that they can control you.

The silent treatment is used by someone brimming over with anger.

Silence is a weapon that can be used to punish, disempower, ostracise, control or to get away from a person or problem. It's a tool of manipulation, as they know silence is an effective way to emotionally manipulate you. It is a form of emotional abuse and vengeance, and you should not accept it. It's of no importance if they harm you; they only care about the power silence gives them, causing you to feel desperate to get back into their good books, to maintain harmony. It is a way of showing they are displeased with you and want to inflict as much suffering as possible.

What you can do

Remember, they are looking to get a particular response out of you. If you refuse to play into their hands, they know better than to try and get you to fall for their ploy again.

- Don't berate yourself and stop thinking it's your responsibility to help this immature person to mature
- Don't retaliate by using the same tactic
- Don't attempt to justify their abusive behaviour, as it's simply not acceptable
- Don't blame yourself; even if you've done something wrong, it is unacceptable to be treated in this way
- Talk to someone you trust so that you can see the situation more clearly
- Let them know you are ready to talk when they are, and leave it at that

'When I am silent, I have thunder hidden inside.' Rumi

Chapter 13

Narcissistic Personality Disorder (NPD)

Are you dealing with someone who has Narcissistic Personality Disorder?

The traits are: lack of empathy for others, manipulation, a sense of entitlement, an inflated sense of their own importance, a deep need for admiration, the need for control, intolerance of views/opinions of others, the inability to appreciate others, lack of awareness or concern about the impact of their behaviour, emotional detachment and more.

Their entire lives are motivated and energised by fear. They worry about being ridiculed, rejected or being wrong. The closer a relationship becomes, the less they will trust. They are afraid you will see their imperfections and judge or reject them. They continually test you with increasingly bad behaviour to find your breaking point. Their fear of being abandoned never seems to dissipate.

They project their anxiety onto loved ones, accusing them of being unsupportive, selfish, negative, or not putting them first or responding to their needs. This is designed to transfer their anxiety, in an attempt to not feel it themselves. As the loved one starts to feel depressed and anxious, the narcissist begins to feel better, stronger and superior.

You cannot reason or use logic with a narcissist when explaining the painful effect their behaviour has. It doesn't make sense to them, as they are only aware of their own thoughts and feelings. Any decision they make is based on how they feel at the time.

Narcissists look towards something, or someone, outside themselves to solve their feelings and needs and expect you to go along with their 'solutions.' They will react with irritation and resentment if you don't.

'Where there is much pride or much vanity, there will also be much revengefulness.'
Arthur Schopenhauer

They lack empathy and tend to be selfish, self-absorbed, manipulative and with a need to be in control. They are rarely apologetic, remorseful or feel guilt. When things don't go well and they feel criticised or less than perfect, they place blame and responsibility on others. Mostly, they blame a particular person, such as their mother or partner, or others who are emotionally attached to them; loving and loyal. People who are close are the safest to blame, as they are least likely to leave or reject them.

Narcissists have to be the best, always in the right, own everything and control everyone. Being at the top gives them a feeling of superiority that makes them feel safe. They have a feeling of entitlement and need constant validation to shore up their fragile self-esteem. No matter how often they are told they are loved, admired or approved of, it is never enough, because deep down, they believe they are unlovable.

'Progress is impossible without change, and those who cannot change their minds cannot change anything.' George Bernard Shaw

What you can do

It helps to distinguish between the two types of narcissism: vulnerable and grandiose.

A vulnerable narcissist's outward shell of self-centredness and self- absorption masks a weak inner core, but a grandiose narcissist believes in their own greatness.

They are masters at manipulation, so appeal to their ego, because if they think your suggestion will benefit them in some way, they will tend to go along with it. If you challenge them, you will never win.

Become aware and recognise that a narcissist will not change their behaviour, as they believe that they are right and you are wrong.

Separate the behaviour from the person and use humour to calm volatile situations. Remain compassionate and non-threatening.

If possible, get as far away from them as you can.

'Your time is limited, so don't waste it living
someone else's life. Don't be trapped by
dogma – which is living with the results of
other people's thinking.' Steve Jobs

Chapter 14

Coercive Control

This is a pattern of behaviour that seeks to remove a person's freedom and strip away their sense of self. Coercive control is a form of psychological abuse; a need for total emotional control over their partner. It is an emotional power move.

The following are common examples of coercive control:

- Isolating you from your family and friends
- Monitoring your activities and movements
- Repeatedly belittling you; calling you names or telling you that you are worthless
- Threatening to harm you
- Threatening to give out derogatory information about you on social media or in other ways
- Damaging your property or personal belongings

The abusive partner usually lacks the confidence to openly discuss, compromise or handle not getting what they want. Coercion can take many forms; it can be aggressive or passive, obvious or subtle, highly toxic or benign.

The abusive partner convinces you that they're totally helpless and rely on you to do everything for them, thus taking away your time and independence and allowing them to gain power over you through their 'reliance.'

Paradoxically, they can make out they are more knowledgeable and better than you at taking charge of everyday happenings and over time, you find that you have lost control of every aspect of your life. You are told they are only trying to help, but at the same time, they work at taking away your independence. They convince you that your friends and family aren't good enough for you, nor are you good at handling your own finances, and other ploys are used to limit your autonomy.

Another sign of coercion is when you find yourself having to tread on eggshells; altering your behaviour and responses so as not to upset them and to avoid their displeasure. You may feel anxious or tense in their presence, unlike when you're with others, or your relationship has a volatility about it, and you feel nervous, scared, exhausted and always on edge.

What you can do

Dealing with the intensity of coercive control can take its toll and you should consider making changes if possible. If you can't get away from them, you should seek professional help to end their manipulation of your emotions, which they use to cover their own inadequacies. Coercive control is unlawful and you can get help and support in dealing with it.

'Because no matter what they say, you always have a choice. You just don't always have the guts to make it.' Ray N. Kuili

Chapter 15

Post-Traumatic Stress Disorder (PTSD)

PTSD is an anxiety disorder caused by events in your life, such as being excluded from your adult child's life, whether directly or through the pressures exerted upon them by a partner and with perhaps the additional loss of not having your grandchildren in your life, bringing further distress, which is very hard to deal with. Often you will have flashbacks and relive the traumatic moments of rejection, with feelings of isolation and abandonment. The impact that estrangement has can be incalculable, affecting every aspect of your life, and cause a breakdown in your mental and physical health.

I have suffered and continue to suffer, from time to time, with PTSD. Some of the symptoms you may have are:

- Nightmares involving being abandoned
- Loss of interest in life and daily activities

- Feeling emotionally numb and detached from other people
- Not having a positive outlook on your future
- Avoiding certain activities, feelings, thoughts and places that can remind you of family occasions and of your grandchildren
- Invasive memories of upsetting scenes or correspondence
- Intense feelings of distress when you think of your alienation

You find that you have mood swings, alternating between blaming yourself or blaming them. You can't get the loss out of your head; estrangement becomes the focal point of your life.

You feel negative about everything and there's no point in anything. You lose interest in the things that you once enjoyed doing. You don't want to see friends. You let things slide and find making decisions increasingly difficult. You try to avoid thinking about your family, as you can't bear to be reminded that you have an adult child and grandchildren whom you no longer see or speak to. You become more fearful of life and what the future might hold.

You have difficulty sleeping; finding it hard to get to sleep or waking up several times throughout the night. You become nervous, tearful and feel irritable for no specific reason. You find your concentration is affected. You feel exhausted. You become solitary.

'Accept yourself, love yourself, and keep
moving forward. If you want to fly,
you have to give up what weighs you down.'
Roy T. Bennett

Chapter 16

Dysfunctional Daughter

When I became estranged from my son and daughter-in-law, I rightly believed that it was generally daughters-in-law who were behind estrangement, but I have since discovered that there is also a high proportion of daughters who initiate estrangement.

Statistics are gravely lacking in the UK, although a small poll by Bristol Grandparents' Support Group (BGSG) showed that 36% of daughters initiate estrangement compared to 23% of daughters-in-law. AGA (Alienated Grandparents Anonymous) in the USA cite the opposite: 43% of daughters-in-law initiate estrangement, compared to 28% of daughters.

Research has found that normally something has happened in the past that prompts a daughter to alienate one or both parents and resolutely lay the blame squarely upon them. Some daughters, upon the death of their father, block their mother from their life and the lives of her grandchildren and give no explanation for their behaviour.

Others, who experienced some kind of trauma in their youth, blame their parents for not protecting them at that time and punish them through alienation when they become independent. There could have been emotional or sexual abuse (perceived or otherwise), differing expectations about family roles, clashes of personality or values and mental health issues. With a daughter, there is a probability that, over time, estrangement can change to become intermittent.

'A hand ready to hit, may cause you great trouble.' Maori saying

Chapter 17

Dysfunctional Son

Overall, there are fewer cases of sons who are estranged from their parents, but when it does happen, it can be for a longer period and can remain permanent.

A son can come to actively dislike his parents due to his inability to cope with his own emotional or mental health issues, or have difficulty relating to his parents. He may feel badly let down or neglected by his parents, or he simply can't face them knowing about his problems.

If a son is living with a partner, he might come under their influence, with demands to break off all connection with his immediate family, causing the estrangement to last the length of that union, or the rest of your life.

'Everyone can master a grief but he that
has it.' William Shakespeare

Chapter 18

Dysfunctional Daughter-in-law

A dysfunctional daughter-in-law is a source of friction in the family. She seeks every opportunity to undermine you. She divides mother and son, withholds grandchildren, controls communication, sabotages family get-togethers and rains misery on one and all; especially her mother-in-law.

She sees you as a bone of contention and a power struggle and it doesn't stop until she can ensure that the relationship between her husband and his mother is fractured. It's a deceptive and gradual process, and often you don't realise it's happened until it's too late. She seeks every opportunity to undermine you.

Her behaviour may well go back to her childhood, in which she might have been in competition with her mother for her father's attention, or she may have seen her mother being uncivil or lacking affection toward her own mother-in-law. Now she's transferred the power struggle to her marriage, with the husband a stand-in for her father and her mother-in-law a competitor for his love.

Alternatively, she might have come from a family that wasn't affectionate, and if her husband's family is more demonstrative, it might make her feel awkward, seeing their closeness.

A further explanation could be, having never developed a sense of self-worth, she's so insecure that she feels anyone in her husband's orbit is a threat. If he has a close relationship with his mother, this cannot be tolerated and must be broken. She becomes increasingly possessive of what she thinks belongs to her and jealous of sharing any part of her life with you.

She needs to feel all powerful and important within the family and wants her mother-in-law to know she is of little or no consequence, as she is number one in her husband's life. Often, she won't say anything directly, but if pressed, she'll find a reason for her behaviour and you will be found as her rival and at fault.

If you try to contact her, she could well ignore you, in an attempt to take away the last shred of family standing you might have, leaving you out in the cold. In other words, cut off. A divisive DDIL is a malicious bully. She could well have a personality disorder.

'All that we send into the lives of others comes
back into our own.' Edwin Markham

Chapter 19

Dysfunctional Son-in-law

In general, whatever issues they have or had with their own parents, there's a good probability they will have them with you. If they felt over-controlled in their childhood or were rejected, demeaned or abandoned, they may view you in the same way and over-react to something you say or do; convincing their partner that you are much more critical and rejecting of them than they realise, thus driving a wedge between you and your adult child.

If estranged from their own parents, they are likely to push your adult child in that direction. When your daughter marries, they marry the psychology of that person and their understanding of family relationships, whether negative or positive. A DSIL can demand that your daughter choose between him and you and the birth of a child can often exacerbate the situation, causing further strain, division and potential estrangement. He could well have a personality disorder.

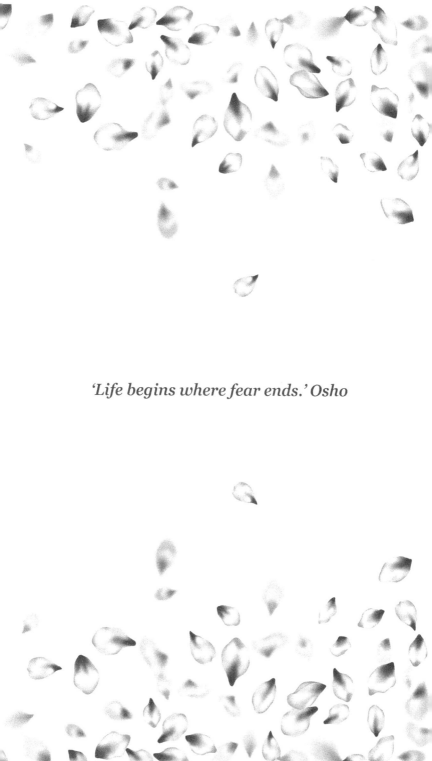

'Life begins where fear ends.' Osho

Chapter 20

The Other Set of In-Laws

When family alienation or estrangement is present, the other set of in-laws often steer clear of the estranged grandparents, so as to safeguard their own relationship with their son or daughter. In the case of a daughter's parents, who are only too happy to welcome the son-in-law into their family, they can easily leave you firmly out of the group. They will not risk their own expulsion by continuing to include you and thereby running the risk of upsetting the status quo.

Grandchildren learn quickly that they have one set of grandparents that they should interact with, either at home or at their grandparents' house. The accepted grandparents attend school functions, are invited on holiday, spend Christmas and share other celebrations with them. They have the grandchildren to stay and in between, they speak to each other and make family visits. Seeing both their mother and father relaxed with only one set of grandparents becomes normal and the children stop asking why their other grandparents are not part of the family.

One lasting memory I have is the christening of my third grandson. When I arrived at the church, I found the accepted grandparents sitting obdurately on the front pew, with my two eldest grandsons lodged between them. They showed little interest in my arrival, nor thought to share our grandsons, by suggesting I sit with them. As they were used to being a sole part of their lives, I don't think it occurred to them that I would want to be, as well. Possibly, it was more prudent simply to ignore me.

Many accepted grandparents are happily at ease not sharing Christmas with the estranged grandparents and you find yourself excluded from all festive family gatherings.

I wrote, one Christmas, to the accepted grandparents and asked if they would agree for Christmases to be shared between us, but my letter was never acknowledged.

Years ago, my son would furtively telephone to wish me happy Christmas while staying at his in-laws. He would be in a room away from the ongoing family celebrations, which meant I wasn't given the opportunity to speak to my grandchildren. I believe they never knew he called me, and his covert telephone call was done to avoid any explanation or disapproval. In time, he ceased calling me altogether. I can only assume he found it easier to ignore the fact that he had a mother, or that I should be part of their Christmas.

*'Be mindful. Be grateful. Be positive.
Be true. Be kind.' Roy T. Bennett*

Chapter 21

Change

Often, estranged parents have an uneasy relationship with change. Change is usually difficult and resolving estrangement can feel out of our control. It can be very scary to consider repairing an estranged relationship, as you're going into untested waters, and it can, indeed, be even more difficult than cutting ties.

Estrangement doesn't normally happen as a result of one big disagreement. It can take years to cut off all contact; a gradual lessening of their presence in your life, of telephone calls, visits and their availability. An exclusion so subtle that, at first, it goes unnoticed and you don't think to question their reasons for not seeing you as often, until it becomes all too apparent that you're no longer welcome and you've been side-lined.

When your life is plagued with unanswered questions, you become intensely conscious of being in a very lonely place, and fear makes its presence known.

Fear is trepidation of the unknown and the uncertainty of the future and how you will cope by yourself. If you have, in addition to estrangement, no family support and old age is looming, it is a frightening prospect that you won't be able to remain independent as you grow older and you ask yourself, 'Who will care for me?' I feel I'm inevitably moving towards an abyss, with the chances of arriving there increasing as every year passes.

'Only in the darkness can you see the stars.'
Martin Luther King Jr

Chapter 22

Mind Control

Can an adult child be brainwashed or mind controlled by their partner?

Having listened to many grandparents' accounts of alienation and read published reports on partner mind control, I believe this plays a big part in estrangement.

Mind control is coercive persuasion. It's about taking away a person's true identity, independence and ability to think critically or logically. It changes their beliefs, attitudes, thinking processes and behaviour.

It's so subtle that the person doesn't realise the slight changes that are happening to their thinking, believing they are still making the decisions, when in fact, the decisions are increasingly being made for them. Because of this, they actively participate in the changes, as they think they are carried out in their best interest. They also don't want to admit that they have been unknowingly manipulated by the person they love and trust.

Mind control is insidious, as it is intended to entrap the recipient and do them harm.

Many parents have a loving and close relationship with their son or daughter up until they meet their partner. As the partner finds their place within the union and gradually becomes dominant and in control – it can happen over a number of years – the adult child lessens contact and distances themselves from the parent. You sense changes to their personality, a certain withdrawal, someone who says little; you find conversation no longer naturally flows between you, and they appear tense in your company. I've seen my son look towards his wife to seek her approval when offered another cup of tea!

When you visit your adult child, they feel compromised; treading on eggshells so as not to upset their partner and to avoid any kind of provocation. They will minimise their conversation and keep to ordinary, everyday subjects that cannot be misconstrued as showing warmth and affection towards you. Talking about work or the children is a safe bet. Reminiscing about occasions prior to the marriage makes the partner feel excluded, and in the effort to prevent further tension, becomes off-limits.

While visiting my son, there would be no opportunity for the two of us to spend any time alone together, and any affectionate hug would be relegated to my arrival and departure; out of sight on the driveway. Our relationship is now dead in the water due, I believe, to the mind control exerted over him. He has been convinced that I am the person at fault and I deserve to be blacklisted.

We no longer talk, text, email or visit each other. The few times I try to connect, he does not respond, and cards in celebration of my birthday or Mother's Day are non-existent. I try to reassure him that he is loved and that I long to renew our relationship, but I get no response. It is as if he's not allowed to think for himself, where I am concerned, and he no longer shows any hint of affection towards me. I feel I'm the enemy within.

Whether the situation will change when my grand-children are no longer living at home remains to be seen. My guess is probably not, as my son has been conditioned over a long period of time and has grown accustomed to life without his mother.

'To live without hope is to cease to live.'
Fyodor Dostoyevsky

Chapter 23

Dominance and Control

Dominance and control constitute emotional abuse and bullying, however obscure.

In the case of a son, he simply becomes less and less involved with you and communication dries up as he goes along with the decisions that his partner makes. Often, men dislike confrontation and refuse to get involved in any kind of dispute, which allows the partner to get her way, and the distancing between him and his parent goes unhindered.

In time, he takes on his partner's negativity towards you and comes to believe that you are the troublemaker. He increasingly believes that his partner wants to have a good relationship with you and you are the person preventing it from happening. This creates resentment and an increasing dislike of you, which then becomes embedded in his mind. Men often prefer to live a life without conflict, especially if there are children involved, and sadly sacrifice their parent for the sake of family unity at home.

A daughter may be involved with a partner who is passive-aggressive or narcissistic and, to lessen friction and protect herself and her children, breaks off her relationship with her parent. Often, it becomes impossible to have contact and the daughter will side with the dysfunctional partner to preserve some semblance of normality in her life. As she becomes increasingly dominated, she rejects all former relationships (this can include siblings and extended family) and is completely under the control of the toxic partner.

The emotions of a grandchild become conflicted by alienation and their relationship with their grandparent is compromised. They quickly learn that communicating with their grandparent is more or less forbidden, as they sense it's not acceptable to the parent. They realise that their grandparent is no longer around or spoken of in the home. It is an effective way of curtailing any kind of connection and lasts throughout their childhood. They lose out on the nurturing love a grandparent can give and the experience influences how they look upon relationships as they mature. For a parent to deprive their child of love because of issues they might have with the grandparent is deplorable.

'Dominance. Control. These things the unjust seek most of all. And so it is the duty of the just to defy dominance and to challenge control.' *Robert Fanney*

Chapter 24

Vindictiveness

The aggrieved adult child or partner can often be malicious and vindictive. They heap their revenge upon you, simply because you exist. Grudge bearing and vindictiveness, for the most part, make for a non-existent relationship. They make life as difficult as possible by ostracising you at every turn.

They try to pit others against you, hoping you will give in, shut up and go away. Normality between you is impossible, as spitefulness runs through their veins.

The aggrieved will stop your grandchildren from having any kind of relationship with you. They will withhold your contact details or convey to their children that connection is not acceptable and any attempt to do so will bring strong disapproval in its wake. They will not be given your presents or letters and you will be blocked from speaking to them, leaving your grandchildren to believe you don't care.

You will be purposely excluded from all family occasions and it is made sure that you are not told about them.

In the case of a vindictive partner, they will avenge your love for your adult child by denying you access to their lives. Vindictiveness is hostile, with evil intent.

'It's not what happens to you,
but how you react to it that matters.'
Epictetus (55-135)

Chapter 25

Loss of Confidence

Loss of confidence is one of the worst aspects of estrangement and can be extremely hard to deal with. Being expelled by your family can be devastating and for many, it rocks the very foundation of their being. Often, we are unable to defend ourselves and respond in a clear and assured manner when challenged.

We feel so undermined that we can't think logically at the time and become tongue-tied, allowing others to dominate the conversation. They appear to have all the answers, which can be disempowering, causing additional feelings of intimidation and vulnerability.

We are so nervous about our inability to effectively speak out when questioned that we become paralysed with fear. This is taken as an admission of guilt on your part, which proves to them that they were in the right all along and allows them to increase their superiority over you. You can liken it to a rabbit caught in the headlights.

At times like these, when you can't defend yourself, you need to draw upon your deepest reserves to survive the onslaught of their deprecation; however unintentional it might be. Try to detach as much as possible and don't attempt to retaliate.

I have found, especially in social circles, that my confidence has plummeted when meeting strangers, which makes meaningful conversation or expressing my opinion in a coherent way more difficult. I find making decisions rather like a minefield and what I thought was the right decision often turns out to be wrong.

Making plans to meet up with friends is stressful, as I never know how I will feel on the day, or whether I will have had a restful night rather than a sleepless one.

Simple things can be overwhelming, which results in not making an effort and leaving things for tomorrow. I get over-anxious and worry about insignificant things; replaying past, present and future scenarios over and over in my head.

To try and counteract negative thoughts, tell yourself that life can change for the better and it can happen when you least expect it. Nothing remains the same for ever.

'Listening to your own heart,
you will start moving in the right direction,
without ever thinking of what is right
and what is wrong.' Osho

Chapter 26

Adversity

The adversity of alienation and estrangement challenges the strongest person and, frequently, many of us don't have the ability to surmount such momentous proportions and feel hopelessly beaten.

Often you are at your lowest ebb and can hardly summon the energy to deal with alienation and estrangement, let alone overcome it.

Adversity will pull you down and destroy you if you allow it to and often, for a certain period, it will seem as if it has won and you are the loser.

What you can do

To overcome adversity, begin by looking at it as an opportunity to strengthen and develop your character so that you become stronger when faced with challenges that may present themselves throughout your life.

Adversity develops your compassion and under-standing for those who are suffering and enables you to help others in need. In turn, this will bring you feelings of validation and being needed, thus decreasing your isolation and despair.

Find a project to get involved in, giving you a sense of purpose that will take you away from thinking about your estrangement and bring you much needed relief. If you have to concentrate on something else, it is impossible to sustain focusing on your estrangement 24/7.

Stay in the moment as much as you can, rather than looking back on how things used to be and focus on anything that is positive in the now. Spend time with people who support and believe in you. Joining a support group can prove invaluable when adversity is knocking at your door.

Recognise that adversity helps you grow and evolve as a person. It increases the substance of who we are. It can be a creator rather than a destroyer.

*'In the ashes of adversity,
lies opportunities.'* S.L. Coelho

Chapter 27

Shame

Some parents who have been shunned by their adult child feel ashamed and mortified that it has happened to them, especially when socialising with those who have a good relationship with their family.

At local events, they don't want others to know of their embarrassing predicament and will keep it secret, brushing off questions in case they are judged or criticised. They think that people will gossip behind their back and they don't dare to disclose that they're no longer in touch with their children or grandchildren.

This truly shows the devastation that adult children heap upon their parents by alienating them. Many parents buy into this propaganda, hook, line and sinker, and subconsciously believe they must have done something wrong to bring about their child's rejection. In other words, they are to blame.

Failure and shame are too hard to make known. They cause feelings of disorientation and the parent cannot sort out or differentiate the reality from the distortion caused by their adult child's actions.

'The Uses of Sorrow.
Someone I loved once gave me
a box full of darkness.
It took me years to understand that this, too,
was a gift.' Mary Oliver

Chapter 28

Right and Wrong

If our children would only live their lives by the bibical concept, 'Do unto others as you would have them do unto you,' the relationship between them and their parents would have the potential to be very different.

I believe that many don't stop to consider the grave injustices they heap upon their parents and have little or no comprehension just how destructive their actions are. They are convinced that they are the ones who have been slighted or wronged and this gives them the moral high ground, a right and the justification to spurn us.

They rationalise that their actions are reasonable and they have no intention of spending time trying to heal the rift, nor on showing compassion or understanding. They are not interested in listening to our point of view; only their opinion matters. Support from other sources further strengthens their resolve and they remain convinced that they are right and you are wrong. It becomes a war of words and there are no winners.

'None are more unjust in their judgments of others than those who have a high opinion of themselves.' Charles Spurgeon

Chapter 29

Toxic Partner

When a powerful, toxic partner succeeds in cutting off all contact with you, along with family members, your adult child will most likely feel that some sort of peace will now prevail in the home, as they have actively chosen to align themselves with their partner, for a variety of reasons.

As they distance themselves from you, the influence of the toxic partner becomes stronger and more insistent. The balance of power and control they've gained leaves them in a position to rule the relationship, placing the accommodating partner in a secondary role. Should your adult child attempt to see or speak to you, the toxic partner will come down even harder, with a cycle of denigration. Failure to manage these psychological bonds can put the marriage at risk.

'An injustice is like a grain of sand in your hand; on its own, its weight may seem insignificant, but injustices have a tendency to multiply, they soon become so heavy that you can no longer bear them.' *Hédi Fried*

Chapter 30

Narratives

I came across these narratives (courtesy of Nancy Lee Klune, www.grandparentsdeniedaccess.com) written by a mother who bears the deep scars of alienation, and who has come to realise that it no longer holds a place in her life. She writes about her painful journey and how she has discovered a new-found sense of being, regaining her self-worth, despite the enormity of being rejected by her only child.

Our journey is ongoing and one has to be mindful each day, so you're not sucked back into a life of despair; the place we all started from.

I am taking my life back

I have given my son and his wife enough of my time, thoughts and sorrow. I have cried enough tears, I have lost enough sleep. I will no longer sacrifice my health, my peace of mind or my vitality at the altar of anger, resentment, hurt and grief

I am bowing out gracefully

I am ready to reclaim my life. It is no longer up for grabs. This is a matter of life or death, and I choose life

I commit myself to peace: peace in my mind, in my speech and in my actions

I am ready for freedom: freedom from melodrama and emotional abuse; freedom to choose happiness that is not dependent on how my son and daughter-in-law treat me

I forgive them and I forgive myself

I now distance myself from harmful, obsessive thoughts and I replace them with thoughts that uplift, heal and love

I now practise gratitude and I transform my life into one of humble thankfulness

I accept that, presently, I am but a shadow in my son's and grandchildren's lives. I understand that that might change with time. No matter what happens, I know that I am safe and loved, and I can accept whatever unfolds

I let go of what I want and I pray for the courage to surrender to what is

I ask for God's grace to live fully, joyously and lovingly

I am taking my life back

Cutting the Cord

We are all born with an umbilical cord that attaches us to our mother. Although it is cut immediately after birth, there is an invisible cord connecting mother and child, resulting in symbiosis. For many, this cord connects mother and child for years, if not a whole lifetime.

I'm not saying this is a bad thing: in a healthy, loving relationship, it can be a source of comfort and joy. Who wouldn't like to be connected, on a deep level, to their child? But, if our adult child cuts us out of his/ her life, we experience a heartache like no other. Unfortunately, some mothers and grandmothers hang on too tightly to this connection, which results in great suffering.

A friend of mine, who is deeply spiritual and very wise, suggested that I cut the cord between me and my son. I've begun doing an exercise every morning, where I imagine a white cord extending from my heart to my son's. I ask angels, spirits and divine guides to please gently dissolve the heartbreaking part of the connection.

By cutting the cord, I don't mean that we close the door to possible healing between us. It is an exercise meant to set us free and give us wings. It's done in the interest of restoring our sanity and helping us heal. It's a way to free ourselves from the angst and devastation that estrangement has wrought in our lives

I've had to face the sad fact that my son has destroyed most of the ties that existed between us. I have had to learn to live without him. I have had to learn to live without the love and connection of family ties – ties that I never dreamed could be torn to shreds.

We cut the cord in the interest of self-preservation and self-love. It doesn't mean that we ever stop loving our child; it means that love for our own life is our priority. It means we stop hanging on to a relationship that is no longer viable and no longer serves us. We get out of harm's way, and we create a space that we can fill with love, acceptance and peace.

Alone

I've always liked having time for myself, to do what I want and just enjoy my own company. During those times, I often feel a creative urge to write, to compose or just listen to music and daydream. It's true that being alone is where magic happens.

Having said that, I have been more alone in the last few years than ever before – a bit too alone. So many heartaches have hindered my capacity and desire to socialise. I used to think that, when I was older, life would become gentler; that because of the attainment of hard-won wisdom, I'd be a loving, grounded and enlightened elder. I never imagined that I would experience so much pain and loneliness in these latter years and find myself flailing and experiencing a bottomless sorrow.

There are days I simply cannot summon up the optimism and hope I've spent years cultivating. I've been diligent in my practice: I am aware of my thoughts and work on improving my state of mind. I work at forgiveness, compassion, optimism and finding purpose. Then, one day, unexpectedly, I experience a lack of energy and a recurrent, pervasive sadness. What happened to all the work I did to manage this kind of melancholy and despair?

I am finding that, after so many years of juggling my emotions and working at mindfulness and positive thinking, I'm rather weary. Any stress I experience seems to affect me to the point of extreme anxiety and bone-heavy exhaustion.

The thing is, after so many years of living in exile from my son and grandchildren, I continue to mourn. It's a bereavement for the living, which never ends. There is no closure, no comfort in grieving the loss of those I love but who don't seem to love me. Yet still I grieve.

I have learned precious lessons. I've learned to let go, to forgive, to detach, to go on with my life. But, if I'm honest, I am war-torn. I have been at war with myself for so long that I wonder if I will ever find real peace. The past haunts me, the future unnerves me and the present is, at least at this moment, difficult.

Tonight, as I write this, I can find no ease, no consolation. But, like everything, this will pass. I will get a good night's sleep, perhaps, or laugh out loud, or take a walk on the beach.

I think many of us can identify with the thoughts of aloneness, as emotions are not static, but ever changing, and so often dependent on other issues of the day, or simply waking up at the start of a new day and feeling a heaviness, for no apparent reason. I can think I'm doing well and have a handle on my son's rejection of me, but every now and then, especially in the evening, the full force of feeling alone hits. I think about what they might be doing *and wonder, what is life all about, when your treasured child and grandchildren, your own flesh and blood, are not in your life? I have found, at times like these, the best antidote is to distract yourself from such emptiness and concentrate on the things in your life that are worthy of your attention.*

Doing My Best

The longer this strange and terrible estrangement goes on, the more blind corners and hairpin turns I come up against. I think I'm doing OK, then I receive a video or see a picture and feel like I'm skidding off the road into a ravine. Yes, I think I'm going on with my life, working at gaining wisdom, compassion and maturity, but there is always the ghost of my missing son and grandchildren haunting me. There are days when I feel enervated, tired, headachy for no apparent reason. I now realise this is brought on by low-lying depression. I usually break down and cry at some point, then eventually the lassitude abates and I resume what has become my new normal, of doing my best to live a full life with a broken heart.

I have prayed, asked for clarity, done my best to learn from all of this. I've read everything I can find on the subject of personal transformation, love, compassion, patience, forgiveness and spirituality. I work diligently on letting go, developing faith in my life, accepting what is and surrendering. I take care of my health, get enough sleep, exercise. I'm a good listener and do my best to be kind and thoughtful. I light candles for my son and grandchildren and, every day, I visualise us together, hugging, laughing and loving each other. I have been in therapy, practised mindfulness, meditated... I'm doing my best.

It just seems that this kind of thing – being abandoned and alienated by my own adult child – has no closure, no resolution. I can't put it behind me, like an argument that ends with insights and mutual understanding. The bridge between us has been destroyed in a fire of confusion and misunderstandings, and it's hell knowing that those I love and miss so much are going on with their lives, on the other side of the chasm.

I have to forgive myself for suffering; for periodically falling into depression. I'm not superhuman – my moods fluctuate, just like the changing weather, the moon or ocean tides. I am doing my best, even on those days when I am sad. I still eat three square meals a day, walk the dog, see friends and go on with life. That's enough to ask of myself – of anyone, really.

It is important, when we feel we are caught in the crosshairs of alienation, that we remind ourselves we are fallible; we're human beings, trying to understand what has happened to us, and how best we can manage our lives in the face of such adversity. At times like this, we should aim to be kind to ourselves and patient with our mixed emotions; allowing them to clear at their own pace.

*'I focused so hard on what I wanted that
I lost sight of what I deserved.'* Unknown

Chapter 31

Abandonment Brings Not Knowing

Being abandoned means you are exiled from the people you hold dearest and from all family activities and the hurt intensifies at the time of seasonal celebrations. One grandmother said that she was already thinking about Christmas during the summertime and didn't know how she was going to get through it alone.

A painful part of abandonment is having no idea, at any given time, where your family are or what they are doing. One Christmas Day, I vainly waited to hear from my son, but his telephone call never came.

In the New Year, when I received a thank you note for gifts I'd sent, my eldest grandson wrote that they'd been away over Christmas in the South Pacific. I remember that it cut me to the quick and I felt a stabbing sensation through my heart as I remembered how I had waited for my son's call, thinking he was in the country. It made me realise that I simply no longer feature in their lives. I play no part in their consciousness.

It took a long time to get over the shock; the fact that my family had travelled over 10,000 miles away and I wouldn't have known if something unforeseen had happened to them. I find the thought heart-rending and it continues to distress me.

'The feeling of abandonment overwhelmed me as I realised that no one had waited, or cared where I was.' *Emily Williams*

Chapter 32

Living Abroad

There are many estranged grandparents who have family that live abroad. Some don't have an address and only know the country of residence. Others do hold an address but are prevented from visiting.

It is impossible to comprehend why a son or daughter can't tolerate seeing their parents periodically, especially when they live in another country and when there are grandchildren. How can anyone be so callous and selfish towards their parents and their own children?

A grandparent I know had, in desperation, travelled abroad in the vain hope of making contact with her estranged daughter and her grandchild, whom she had never met. On arriving at the house, she found that they had left and was told they would not return until she had gone away.

Often, grandparents live on an empty promise that at some obscure time in the future they will be permitted to see their grandchildren. No arrangement is fixed and it is usually dependent on some other happening, real or imagined, and the visit never comes to fruition. Such behaviour can be compared to a cat with a mouse.

We can only assume that our adult children have little or no comprehension of the abject misery, pain and humiliation they cause and for whatever reason, you are of no importance to them as they severe all links.

'In the end, only three things matter: how much you loved, how gently you lived, and how gracefully you let go of things not meant for you.' *Gautama Buddha*

Chapter 33

Strangers

As your grandchildren grow up and you possess no current photographs of them, you have little idea what they look like. They could pass you by on the street and you wouldn't know. The realisation of such a thing is beyond all belief and yet, in my case and in many others, it's true.

When my grandsons were young, I received an individual school photograph of each child at Christmas, but over time, my daughter-in-law stopped sending them. Recently I came across a family holiday photograph on Instagram. It was like looking at strangers, when you know they're not. You instinctively feel they're off-limits and you have no rights. It's like you're trespassing in a place you don't belong.

A huge chunk of your life has been wiped out; it no longer exists. It occurred to me that I might not even know if my son had a life-threatening illness or if he had died. Chillingly, it would be up to his wife to decide if or when I should be told.

'Nothing is lost that love remembers.'
Kate McGahan

Chapter 34

Social Media

Social media can be a blessing or a curse. For grandparents who have a good relationship with their grandchildren, it can be a great way to keep in touch, sending messages to each other and sharing photographs, but for grandparents who are estranged, it is very different.

Searching for your grandchildren on social media can be difficult, and if you find them, it doesn't mean you are automatically in touch. One grandchild I am in contact with responds haphazardly to the few simple messages I've sent, and this can become really stressful, as being estranged means you are constantly aware of the possibility of further rejection. If you don't hear from them, you feel as if you've gone back to square one and you naturally begin to fear that they don't want to know you.

Seeing photographs of family holidays, celebrations that you know nothing about and not recognising faces is hard. On the other hand, being able to 'see' them is a joy, and having a small glimpse into their lives is, for me, worth the apprehension one might feel.

'*Staying separate from those
we love hurts.*' *Jodi Aman*

Chapter 35

Cards and Gifts

Many grandparents whose cards and gifts go unacknowledged or have been told they are not wanted and won't be passed on keep a celebratory box where they place written cards, letters and gifts never sent, in the hope of giving the contents to their grandchildren when they become adults. One day, it will be a way of showing our lost grandchildren that they were never forgotten during the intervening years of silence.

Other grandparents open a savings account and religiously put money in, so their grandchildren can benefit when they are no longer minors. Others, whose grandchildren are still very young, leave a gift in their will. It is an empowering act and a way to maintain a connection.

'Honesty is the first chapter in the book of wisdom.' Thomas Jefferson

Chapter 36

Loneliness

Estrangement and alienation bring loneliness. Your heart is empty and there is a limitless void that can never be filled unless your child returns to you.

I just want my son back. I need the affection and love that we both once held dear. I need to see his face, his smile, and hear his laughter. His dry sense of humour, his dignity and honesty, his gentleness, his quiet way and kindness; all of which are etched in my memory. I also need to be his proud mother and for people to know he's my son.

I want to spend time with him, to share that similarity we hold in being mother and son. In our DNA, we have a uniqueness that no one, however hard they try, can take away from us. I believe he wants to live in harmony and that deep down in his heart, the love he once felt for his mother lies dormant. I believe he suffers as well, but simply doesn't know how to make his way back.

'The only way out of the labyrinth of suffering is to forgive.' John Green

Chapter 37

Sadness

Sadness is like a heavy black cloak that is all encompassing and all enduring. For as long as you are banished from your adult child's life and the lives of your grandchildren, it brings profound sadness. It can be a constant or a subtle background heaviness that casts its dark shadow over you. Its presence is there from the moment you wake up. It's not something you can shake off, as it is worn like a mantle. You can find that your emotions change from feelings of relative calm to despair, from one minute to the next.

Often, it only takes one small thing to spark sadness. It's a companion whose presence you don't want or need in your life. Sadness comes from a happening you didn't expect, a grave loss and a sense of powerlessness to change the status quo.

'Don't cry when the sun is gone,
because the tears won't let you see the stars.'
Violeta Parra

Chapter 38

Heartbreak

It is said that one can die of a broken heart. The loss of your living adult child can break your heart in two, as you feel there is little or nothing to live for. The additional loss of your grandchildren compounds the situation.

Now, more so than in previous times, societies across the world increasingly see people living on their own, and when alienation is part of your life, it is doubly hard to bear. Your support system has been pulled from under you, knowing that your adult child is no longer part of your life. Emotional security has been swept away. Friends are supportive, but they're not family. There is a difference, no matter how one tries to think otherwise. Blood, we are told, is thicker than water, but with estrangement, this proves not to be true.

You find that nothing makes sense. The tapestry of generations becomes meaningless. When your heart breaks, it leaves you vulnerable and with feelings of impotency and knowing that life will never be the same. Life is full of broken hearts; it's something that happens to the majority of people at one time or another. You are not alone in the tragedy of heartbreak.

'As water reflects the face, so one's life
reflects the heart.' Proverb 27:19

Chapter 39

Trust

When you have been ostracised by the most loved person in your life, how do you learn to trust again?

If your adult child abandoned you because you no longer fitted into their life, or you didn't act according to their expectations, then why shouldn't someone else do the same? A wrong move, a wrong word, could find you alone again.

Learning to put your trust in a new relationship can be a painstakingly difficult journey to make. Trusting someone means you believe them to be reliable, you feel confident about them, and you feel safe; physically and emotionally.

Trustworthiness is one of the most enriching and rewarding feelings between people. To trust again, I believe you have to start by rebuilding your shattered sense of self.

Begin by knowing yourself and believe you have much to give to those who recognise your true worth. Realise you're not a lesser person with your adult child out of your life, and start to think of them with compassion and forgiveness, so that you can release them and yourself and begin to move away from the grave hurt they have caused you. At such a time, you can begin to learn to trust again. If you think you can protect yourself by continuing to mistrust and not take people as you find them, you will block potentially worthwhile relationships.

Before a parent accepts an offer from their adult child to mend the relationship, they should consider whether it's what they really want.

- Are you able to trust and go forward without anger or resentment for the initial wrongdoing and for all the pain and suffering you've endured, often over a prolonged period of time?
- Can you manage to have a healthy and rewarding relationship again with your adult child and partner, by leaving out any blame?
- Are you able to forgive them?
- Do you trust the reasons why they have had an apparent change of heart?
- Can you cope with occasional aspersions and slights?
- Has too much been destroyed over the years?
- Have you moved on to such an extent that you are happier without them in your life?

Only you can decide whether it is worthwhile to take the risk and go into the precarious unknown, where rejection could happen again.

'There comes a time in your life when you
have to choose to turn the page, write
another book or simply close it.'
Shannon L. Alder

Chapter 40

Belonging

One of the many destructive elements that surrounds alienation is realising that you no longer belong in a family that you used to be a pivotal part of. As time passes and estrangement increases, it erodes all sense of belonging. You are no longer welcome and often you're seen as an intruder and therefore a threat.

- Belonging supports who we truly are, and when it is absent, you feel adrift from the very fabric of life
- Belonging means acceptance as a member or a part of something. It's one of the main social structures of society

To accept someone, you make room for change, while alienation represents rigidity and the inability and unwillingness to do so.

What we can do is embrace self-acceptance, stand up for ourselves and move forward, allowing ourselves to grow and evolve, instead of fighting against no longer belonging. We do not need another person's approval to survive. Focus on and be kind and loving to yourself, and know that, deep within, we are all connected to the universe. We are all one.

'Yes, I am imperfect and vulnerable and sometimes afraid, but that doesn't change the truth that I am also brave and worthy of love and belonging.' Brene Brown

Chapter 41

Ups and Downs

There is no rhyme nor reason for how one will feel as each day dawns. Some are recovery days, with positive energy and a zest for life; wanting to achieve things, however small or mundane. The world can look and feel good again and it brings a spring to your step. Another day, you are despairingly low. When this feeling hits, I find I don't want to see anyone and usually stay in the sanctuary of my home.

I spend time with my two cats, who comfort me with their presence. I sit or potter in the garden. I read and play music, cook something nutritious or just have a cup of tea! Nurturing and healing are needed on low days. I no longer try to 'snap out of it' or 'pull myself together,' but quietly acknowledge that there are times when self-kindness and care are needed. I allow myself just 'to be' knowing that the melancholy will lift and pass.

'Have courage for the great sorrows of life
and patience for the small ones; and when
you have laboriously accomplished your
daily task, go to sleep in peace.' Victor Hugo

Chapter 42

Grief

Grief is a longing for something or someone who is no longer in your life. Grief never leaves you, but changes in intensity as time passes and slowly it becomes less oppressive. Time is not necessarily a healer, because grief stays alongside you; it accompanies you, no matter where life takes you. It is in the background, coming to the fore when least expected. It is a profound sense of loss, of yearning, of hopelessness. It's the loneliest feeling in the world, as you feel empty, alone and unwanted.

The seven stages of grief are

- Shock and denial
- Pain and guilt
- Anger and bargaining
- Depression, reflection and loneliness
- Upward turn (lifting of depression)
- Reconstruction (trying to find realistic solutions)
- Acceptance and hope

Grief is a natural process and is more difficult when the person you love has left your life but hasn't died. The more significant the loss, the more intense your grief will feel. Grieving takes different forms; some of us grieve openly, others try to hide their feelings of grief. Some grieve for a few weeks or months, others do so for years; even the rest of their lives. It depends on your coping mechanism, your character, your life experience, your spiritual beliefs and how much that lost person meant to you.

Talking about the loss can put you on the road to recovery. Expressing your fundamental feelings helps you to pass through this devastating period and will give you valuable support at a vulnerable time. It will also help soothe the confused and painful emotions that you are faced with.

Support groups are really helpful in sharing your sorrow with others who have experienced similar losses, and where you find non-judgemental and empathetic support. The realisation that you are not alone, and that you don't need to suffer in silence, can kick start the healing process.

It is vital, during this time of grief, that you value yourself, by taking care of your wellbeing, exercising in moderation, eating healthily and resting as often as you can. Remember to be kind to yourself.

'Grief never ends... But it changes.
It's a passage, not a place to stay.
Grief is not a sign of weakness,
nor a lack of faith...
It is the price of love.' Unknown

Chapter 43

Fear

Fearing fear is one of the companions of alienation and estrangement. It is hard to cope with fear when you feel neglected and unwanted. If you allow fear to get a grip, your life can become unbearable, as fear constantly asks, 'What if?' 'What if nothing changes?', 'What if you never see or speak to your adult child again?', 'What if you fall sick or have an accident; who will be there for you?' Fear takes away peace of mind and diminishes enjoyment of life. It will occupy your thoughts and the four corners of your mind, if you allow it.

Fear has a large part to play in estrangement and once it gets a foothold, it stealthily establishes itself in the mind and becomes a major hurdle to overcome, as it is at ease with anger, avoidance, shame, confusion, uncertain boundaries, defensiveness, paralysis and running away.

When we can sit with fear and ride it safely to the other side, we learn that we can survive our worst fears and we're able to change and move on; out of the paralysis that so many are trapped in.

I found that fear caused me to withdraw from others. I found I didn't want to leave the four walls of my home. I felt depressed and very sad, often breaking down in tears, as I felt everything was futile. I lost my confidence and felt no one cared.

Betrayal by those we love can have a prolonged and profound impact on our emotional state, which can affect us for years; filling us with self-doubt, feelings of emptiness and being afraid.

Fear can come from thoughts of failure and believing you're not good enough to be loved. It attacks the very essence of you and it can take a monumental effort not to succumb.

- If you struggle with the fear of loss, you will continue to face feelings of abandonment
- If you fear rejection, you will attract people who do not respect or appreciate your value
- If you fear commitment and emotional vulnerability, your heart will keep breaking until it learns to love
- If you fear losing control, you will keep facing circumstances that are uncontrollable
- If you fear death, you will constantly be reminded about the futility of attachment and the impermanence of everything

What you can do

When fear triggers itself, take some deep, slow, calming breaths and repeat out loud that you are safe and the fears are all in your head. I find that speaking out loud is helpful at times of severe anxiety, and I try to concentrate on all the positive things in my life, such as having a roof over my head, enough food to eat and money to get by. I remind myself of my good health, the people who do care about me, the freedom and stability I have in my life.

Distract your mind with an action such as singing, reciting poetry or reading out loud, preventing your mind from spending time on the 'what ifs.'

I stop myself dwelling on what I don't have, or what might happen to me, by keeping in the present moment, rather than going back to the past or thinking about the future. No one knows for sure what the future holds, and all we can do is live in the present moment.

If one of your fears comes stalking, trust that you will meet it with your strength of character at the time and know that it won't destroy you. Use a mantra such as 'I am safe, I am strong,' and repeat it on a daily basis or whenever needed.

'Our anxiety does not empty tomorrow of its sorrows, but only empties today of its strengths.' Charles H. Spurgeon

Chapter 44

Letting Go

One way to survive alienation is to let it go. This doesn't mean you let go of a quiet hope that, someday, your adult child will return to you, but you let go of the hurt, the demeaning way in which you were deserted, your exclusion from your family, the tears you shed, and all the emptiness and despair this has brought you.

Letting go isn't easy, because it's a loss you've held on to for years, hoping alienation could somehow right itself and come to an end. Being able to let go is an act of self-love, as you begin to gain your life back; you're regaining your sense of self. You are gaining the ability to allow yourself to let go, so that you can focus on building yourself up and learning to love yourself again, knowing you are worth it.

When your adult child makes not the smallest move towards reconciliation, and you cling blindly to the hope that they will, this keeps you stuck and unable to move forward. It prevents you from making the effort to change your life for the better. You will not be in a healthy and balanced state, if and when reconciliation presents itself; rather you will be that broken and bitter person, unable to embrace any new changes that come into your life.

By letting go, you will start to grow as a person, attracting new people into your life and you will find that better things come your way. It's a tough call and you can only follow through when the time feels right. By having the courage to let go, you can gain so much.

'When one door closes another one opens;
but we often look so long and so regretfully
upon the closed door that we do not see
the one that has opened for us.'
Alexander Graham Bell

Chapter 45

Deprivation

One of the most grievous aspects of estrangement is being deprived of giving your love freely to your adult child and grandchildren. You are robbed of the most basic of human emotions, when prevented from showing your love to your own kin. A parent's love for their child and grandchildren, whatever their age, never diminishes, as they are part of the very essence of your life. Not being allowed to give your love leaves you joyless and broken-hearted.

Recently I came across a photograph of my adult child and was shocked to see how unwell and unhappy he looked. I immediately wanted to go to him, put my arms around him, offer him comfort and somehow reassure him that all would be well.

Alienation brings deprivation to both mother and adult child. It's heartless and cruel.

A grandmother I know who has been stopped from meeting her grandson said it was devastating to think that she had already missed out on his various stages of development, from newborn, through babyhood, first words, first steps and into toddlerhood.

Ahead of her stretches a bleak future of deprivation, as she knows she will miss him starting primary school or see him act in school plays. She will not be there to help when needed, whether on occasion or regularly, or see him develop through the years.

It is even more painful to know that the other set of grandparents are part of her grandson's life, enjoying all she is deprived of. She doesn't know if her grandson is even aware of her existence, or will ever know the love she holds for him.

Deprivation stops you from sharing in your grandchildren's scholarly and sports achievements and you are prevented from sharing important birthdays such as their 16th, 18th and 21st.

As time goes by, you miss out on their graduation and even marriage or the birth of great grandchildren. It's a huge disservice that has been done to us, as our role of grandparent has been wilfully stolen from us.

'I should know enough about loss to realize
that you never really stop missing
someone – you just learn to live around
the huge gaping hole of their absence.'
Alyson Noel

Chapter 46

Love

We love our estranged adult children simply because they are our children, despite the chasm that they have created and which exists between us. My personal experience of alienation has found me on a road I never thought I'd have reason to travel along.

Besides bringing deep unhappiness and leading me to the brink of despair, it has slowly taught me to be compassionate and have empathy for the suffering of others. I have found, surprisingly so, that rather than resent my son for the carelessness he continues to show, I feel a constant well of love and compassion and I know that whatever comes my way, nothing and nobody can change the feelings I have for him. I find this to be a great source of comfort and it dispels the need to fight back; to blame and criticise. I've found it has created a patience within that helps me live with not having him in my life at this given time.

In life, people don't necessarily act as you would want. They disappoint you, they hurt you; but that doesn't mean you need to stop unconditionally loving them. Suffering has brought a heightened awareness to me which, indirectly, has been a gift from him to me. I believe that every situation is meant and every situation has a reason.

When there is love, no words need to be spoken. Love can be conveyed through action; a silent look, the smallest deed. Love is infinite. It can be sensed and felt. Love is the key to open all doors and it breaks down all barriers. It has no limits.

'A mother loves her children unconditionally. However they wrong her, she'll carry on loving them.' Alaa Al Aswany

Chapter 47

Kindness

Kindness is an act straight from the heart. It spreads happiness and fills the recipient with joy. The act of kindness rebounds on you; it makes you feel good about yourself, as the smallest gesture can have a profound effect. It comes free, and anyone can give or receive kindness.

Showing kindness can change a person's life by giving them hope, lifting them up when they are down and letting them know they are not alone.

Kindness gives that extra boost, often when needed the most and is always positive. An act of kindness remains in the memory forever. Everyone needs kindness in their life and when it comes, it's a gift from heaven.

Estrangement and alienation have no room for kindness. Both are too busy pulling you down and making you feel as bad as possible. They are the opposite of kindness. This doesn't mean, however, that given the opportunity, we can't continue to show kindness towards our abuser. Doing so might make them think about their acts of unkindness towards us and start to bring change, for the betterment of both.

'Kindness is the language which the deaf can hear and the blind can see.' *Mark Twain*

Chapter 48

Forgiveness

When you have been treated unfairly by your adult child and they have taken it upon themselves to disown you, barring you from their lives as well as your grandchildren's, often with little or no explanation for their actions, you are left feeling completely lost. You desperately wonder where you went wrong and how you can put it right.

As time passes, you realise that you can't mend the broken pieces on your own and there is little you can do to bring your adult child back into your life. All you can do is live your life as best you can and learn to forgive them.

By forgiving their heartlessness, you release yourself from the pain and sadness that has been inflicted and you will find that your estrangement is no longer the focal point of your life.

Forgiveness does not mean that you condone their actions; it simply means you have released yourself from the drama that has been created. You have let go of your grievances and judgements so that you can move towards healing yourself.

But how do you forgive someone who has wounded you to the quick? How do you forgive, and free yourself from self-judgement? Forgiveness isn't easy and we are not always ready to do it, but it is a healing balm for the hurt we feel and essential for our wellbeing, as it sets us free from the burden of anger, resentment and estrangement.

Forgiveness takes courage and trust in the goodness of others. It allows you to open your heart when your adult child continues to levy pain upon you while their heart remains closed.

When you can offer forgiveness to the person who has wronged you, it will bring you peace within, and with this comes self-healing. Forgiveness frees us from the constraints of the past, leaving the injury behind, so that you can live life in the now.

Forgiveness isn't something you do for the person who has wronged you; it's something you do for yourself.

'On the wings of forgiveness is carried all other wisdom.' Honey J. Rubin

Chapter 49

Opening the Window

You cannot second guess your adult child's perception of and behaviour towards you, but you can become pro-active and turn to the positive things in your life. If you are convinced there is nothing good in your life, then start to think about developing your spiritual knowledge by learning about the wisdom of ancient and modern sages.

I started on my spiritual path over thirty years ago, when, knowing nothing about spirituality, I came across the writings of Edgar Cayce on a friend's bookshelf. As I began to read, it was as if a window had opened inside my mind and the sunlight came flooding in. It was a whole new dimension that I had no idea existed. Every book of wisdom I've since read has been a stepping-stone, helping me find the strength to face the obstacles that have presented themselves and has offered me much needed comfort along the way. The new found knowledge helped me to discover my propensity for compassion and empathy and an ability to forgive people who have hurt me and realise that their behaviour stems from their own unhappiness and inadequacies.

When you expect others to heal your pain, it can't happen, as healing comes from within; in other words, from your higher consciousness. Connecting to it gives you a tranquillity, an emotional stability, and you lose the need to retaliate. You will find that you can 'let go' of another person's rancour and petty mindedness while continuing to remain grounded and calm. They can no longer harm you.

Begin every day feeling positive and grateful for all that you might have in your life; good health, a home, enough money to pay the bills and feed yourself, people who care about you, your loyal pet that shares their life with you. In addition, think of the fresh air you breathe, the sunshine, the rain that falls, the majestic sky, the trees, the green fields and the birds. Think of a mantra that you can recite every day. Louise Hay has many in her book, You Can Heal Your Life.

Take five minutes out each day to sit quietly, slowly inhaling and exhaling, releasing the tensions in your body, while concentrating your eyes on an object so that you learn to still the endless chatter in your head. It will help you to control your thoughts, so that you don't lapse into those of your estrangement. It will give you a restful break from your unhappiness.

Healing yourself does take conscious effort and time. There is no magic formula, but the sooner you begin, the quicker your pain will stop, or at least diminish to the degree that it's no longer all-consuming and the focal point in your life. Learn about calmness, forgiveness and compassion; without which you will remain a prisoner of despair. Talk to someone who has faced hard times in their own life and learn how they managed to overcome these. It will give you fortitude and help you realise that you are not alone and that people are often faced with the same trauma of loss. More importantly, it will help you realise that you, too, can survive whatever you come up against.

'Today I choose to live with gratitude for the love that fills my heart, the peace that rests within my spirit and the voice of hope that says all things are possible.' Anonymous

Chapter 50

Change Your Belief System

To help bring an end to your suffering, you need to change the beliefs that are central to your estrangement. The absence of your adult child's presence and the affection that they once showed must be counterbalanced with love so that you can survive the ravages of rejection.

Beliefs are merely thoughts that can be changed. What are you thinking now? That your life won't and can't change unless your adult child comes back to fill the void they left? Do you want this thought to dominate the rest of your life? If so, you will never find happiness again.

The point of power is now, so this moment is when you start changing your beliefs. No matter how long you've held negative thoughts that have affected your happiness and wellbeing, you can be free from them right now...

As long as you spend your precious life feeling sad, you continue to punish yourself. The more you depend on this pattern of thinking, where your adult child is concerned, the more you will fear your loss. They won't be aware of your suffering; the only person who is, is you.

As you continue to limit positive thoughts, the good things in life won't find their way towards you.

The first step to recovery is to actually care about yourself. To love, approve and accept yourself exactly as you are. Know that you are good enough.

We must cease criticising ourselves, as this keeps us locked into negative thought and blocks change for the better. Once we decide to actively approve of ourselves and accept that we are alright as we are, our positivity will attract positive people and situations to our lives. No longer will there be a place for negativity. Believe that you are deserving of only the best that life wants to offer you.

'I breathe in love and I flow with life.'
Louise L. Hay

Chapter 51

Affirmations and Visualisations

To continue with your recovery, daily affirmations can play a large part in regaining your wellbeing. Recite your affirmations out loud, looking in the mirror and speak in the present tense, not in the future. You can also write down each affirmation several times, followed by repeating them slowly and clearly.

- I am willing to change and grow
- All is well in my world. I am always safe
- I am creating a new way of thinking
- I am worth loving
- I am powerful
- I open myself to all good
- I deserve the best
- I deserve love
- I am receptive
- I am motivated by love

Louise Hay writes in You Can Heal Your Life:

'I forgive everyone, including myself.

When I hold on to the past with bitterness and anger and don't allow myself to experience the present moment, I am wasting today. If I hold on to bitterness and grudges for a long time, it has to do with forgiving myself, not the other person. If I hold on to old hurts, I punish myself in the here and now. I no longer want to sit in a prison of self-righteous resentment. I decide that I'd rather be happy than always right. I forgive myself and stop punishing myself.'

Visualisations are when you simply visualise what you want in your life. Before you begin, write down your goals and the emotions you would feel if you had already achieved them.

Put aside about thirty minutes in which you won't be disturbed and sit or lie quietly, as it's important you are relaxed. To begin, concentrate on your breathing by taking slow, deep breaths in and out, at the same time focusing on the different parts of your body, starting from your toes to the top of your head. Notice how the tension is leaving each part of your body as you move from place to place, and a feeling of relaxation and calmness takes over. Take your time to do this exercise, which should take several minutes. Don't be tempted to rush it or not do it. When you feel ready, begin to imagine the goals you listed, one by one, and see yourself enjoying your new-found happiness; all the time going deeper into the feeling, allowing these wonderful, positive emotions to envelope you. Experience exactly how you would feel if your dreams had come true. You will no doubt feel joy, happiness, confidence and a sense of freedom.

Try to see your emotions as the language that communicates your goals to your sub-conscious. The pictures are there to show you what to look out for as you reach for your goal, and the emotions and feelings are for the benefit of your brain. The more you practise visualisation, the more effective it will become and the quicker you will leave the present negativities of your life behind.

'The future depends on what we do in the present.' Mahatma Gandhi

Chapter 52

Focus on the Present

When there is estrangement in your life, you tend to look towards the future. We live our lives in the hope that someday, things will change for the better. We'll see our adult child and grandchildren again; we will somehow get back a meaningful relationship with them. Things will come right... in the future.

When our energies are focused on the future, we prevent ourselves from being fully alive and enjoying the present moment. As long as we are wrapped up in thinking about what might happen, we lose our ability to grasp what is on offer now and the opportunities that might enter our life pass us by. Living your life stuck in the past or concentrating on what might happen in the future leaves the present moment empty, and you sad.

The only time that exists is the present moment and this is the only time you can live your life. The future belongs to our imagination.

'If you want to be happy, do not dwell in the past, do not worry about the future, focus on living fully in the present.' Roy T. Bennett

Chapter 53

Positive Side of Suffering

How can there be a positive side of suffering? There is, if you can take one step back and observe the person you are now. Suffering often brings positivity as it allows for a deeper level of awareness, and our capacity for empathy deepens. We find we can relate to other people's unhappiness, and we have a clear vision of how they feel when adversity presents itself. Often, we can support them through the hurdles and difficulties they face, as we know how it feels.

Suffering develops humility and gratitude for the good things that come your way. You appreciate the smallest of kind gestures, the simplicity of nature. You look beyond the material aspects for things that carry the true meaning of life.

Suffering makes us stronger and we are left wiser and more confident and capable than ever before.

For me, personally, I have found a new strength in practising meditation and turning towards my spiritual beliefs to see the bigger picture, which continues to help me develop my own humanity.

The ones that cannot love us back are those that, ultimately, remind us that we are worthy of love. They highlight all of our insecurities and teach us to let go of what does not serve our higher purpose.

Forgive the people who have hurt you, because they are our greatest teachers. The suffering they cause brings a new-found intuition and a greater sense of integrity.

They teach us emotional resilience, mental strength, compassion and courage. Be grateful to them, as the abuser is an example of what we should resist becoming.

'Gratitude is not only the greatest of virtues,
but the parent of all the others.' Cicero

Chapter 54

Our Grandchildren

So where do grandchildren figure in your estrangement and alienation by your adult child? Besides parents being deprived of love from their adult child, grandchildren are deprived of a relationship with their grandparents.

My grandsons are all young men and it is apparent that they don't know how to relate to a grandmother they barely know. I can sense they are unsure of what to say or do and are still, in many ways, conditioned by years of minimal contact, which creates guilty feelings of going against their mother if they respond and would like to get to know me. I tread gingerly, trying to preserve what little connection I have and at the same time, try to reach out to develop a closer bond.

I'm concerned that their long-enforced estrangement will affect any future close relationships they may have, as being caught up in their parents' estrangement with their grandmother has clearly had an impact on them; especially throughout their formative years.

I hope, in time, that things will improve, we will be able to get to know each other and find a way to mend the broken ties and gradually we will share a heartfelt warmth and affection, which will also embrace future spouses and children.

'Love is the bridge between you and everything.' Rumi

Chapter 55

Afterthoughts

Beyond All Belief came out of my own personal pain and suffering, having lost the person I value most in my life. I believe that when adversity presents itself, it is a teacher, on many levels, and if you are able to take one step back from the emotional turmoil it creates, you can turn it into something positive; for yourself and others.

Being given the opportunity to use my experiences for the betterment of all is truly a gift in itself. It takes time to reach a point where you can look at loss in a positive light, but by drawing on the power of your inner self and looking within, it is possible to do.

Letting go of blame and willingly forgiving the person or persons who have hurt you the most is the first step towards freeing yourself from the bonds of resentment and unhappiness. You will never be able to go forward in your life unless you take this important step. If you continue to stay stuck in the past, that is where you will remain, and you will forego any enriching opportunities that might come your way.

I know all too well how devastating it is to be cast aside by your adult child, but how vitally important it is to turn the heartache and sadness into a life worth living.

I hope *Beyond All Belief* gives you the tools to take those first tentative steps and helps you on your path of renewal. It comes with love and compassion.

'Find the love you seek, by first finding the
love within yourself. Learn to rest in that
place within you that is your true home.'
Sri Sri Ravi Shankar

**From Tao Te Ching
(Lao Tzu)**

'I have just three things to teach:
simplicity, patience and compassion.
These three are your greatest treasures.
Simple in actions and in thoughts,
you return to the source of being.
Patient with both friends and enemies,
you accord with the way things are.
Compassionate towards yourself,
you reconcile all beings in the world.'

Prayer of St. Francis
(associated with Saint Francis of Assisi)

'Lord, make me an instrument of thy peace
Where there is hatred, let me sow love
Where there is injury, pardon
Where there is doubt, faith
Where there is despair, hope
Where there is darkness, light
And where there is sadness, joy

Oh Divine Master, grant that I may not so much seek
to be consoled, as to console
to be understood, as to understand
to be loved, as to love

For it is in giving that we receive
It is in pardoning that we are pardoned
and it is in dying that we are born to eternal life.'

Recommended Books of Comfort

Christina Feldman – *Compassion*. Rodmell Press

Kahlil Gibran – *The Prophet*. William Heinemann Ltd

Louise Hay – *Inner Wisdom*. Hay House Inc

Louise Hay – *You Can Heal Your Life*. Hay House Inc

Eckhart Tolle – *The New Earth*. Penguin Books

About the Author

Diana began her journey of estrangement many years ago. As time passed and her despair grew she founded a grandparent support group which led to her writing *Beyond All Belief.*

Overcoming her own family adversity remains a work in progress.

Diana lives in Oxfordshire, UK with Bella her feline companion. She can be contacted at oxfordshiregsg@gmail.com

Lightning Source UK Ltd.
Milton Keynes UK
UKHW021015210620
365275UK00009B/606

9 781786 236845